DEDICATION

To David

Lil' LIBROS
www.LilLibros.com

Wepa
Published by Little Libros, LLC

Text © 2023 Danielle J Montalvo
Art © 2023 Danielle J Montalvo
Designed by Haydeé Yañez

Library of Congress Control Number 2022935551

Printed in China

Fourth Edition – 2023   JHP 04/23
28 27 26 25 24 23   4 5 6 7 8 9 10
ISBN 978-1-948066-54-9

Mia Emilia Lucia Renata considers herself quite exceptional, among all things. She is...

Mia Emilia Lucia Renata se considera bastante excepcional, entre todas las cosas. Ella es...

...fashionable...

...amante de la moda...

...creative...

...creativa...

...and smart.

...e inteligente.

$1+1=2$

Mia Emilia

$$\begin{array}{r} 12 \\ \times 4 \\ \hline 48 \end{array}$$

But not everyone appreciates genius.

Pero no todo el mundo aprecia la genialidad.

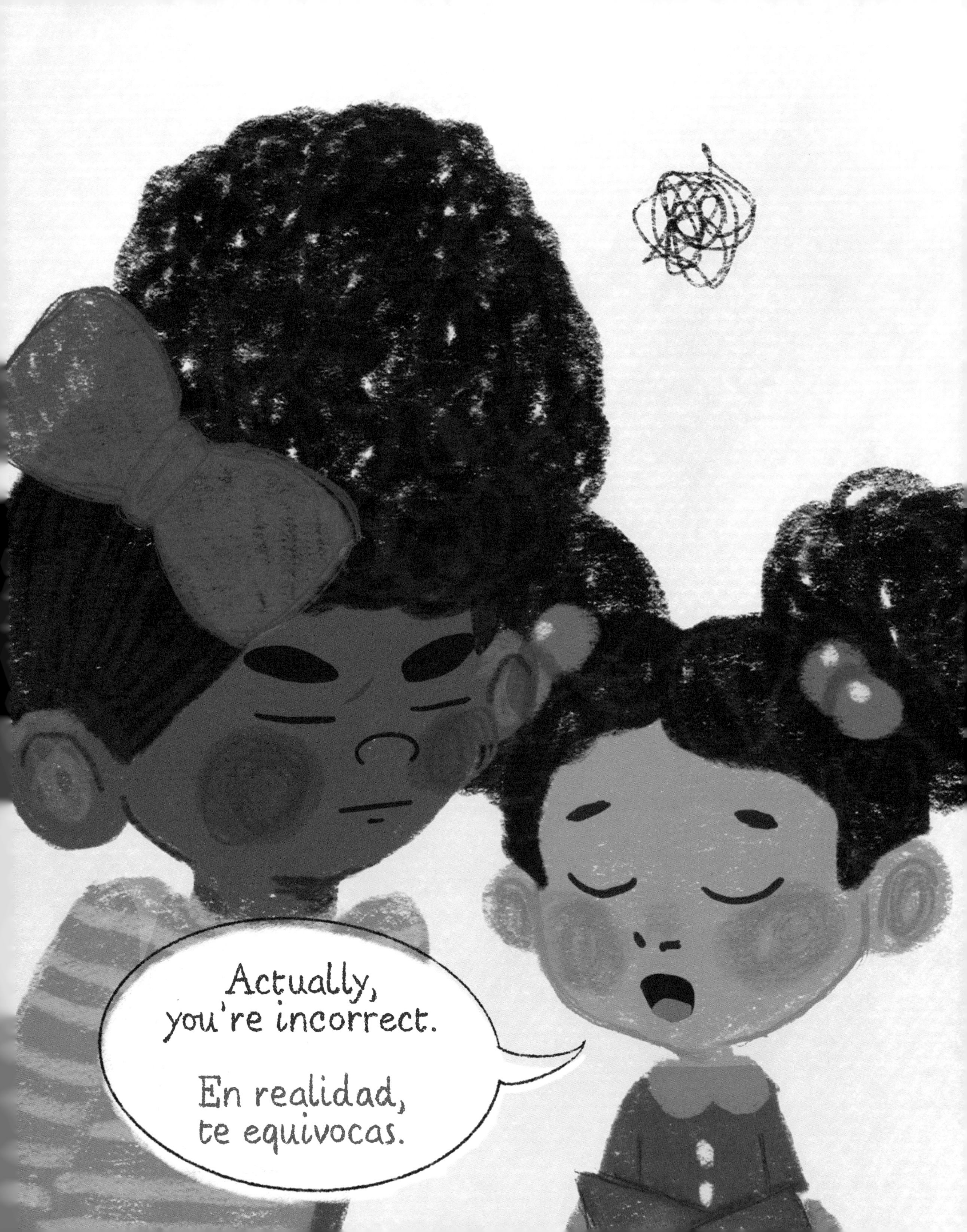
Actually, you're incorrect.
En realidad, te equivocas.

Her teachers say...

Su maestra dice que...

She's too clumsy!

¡Es muy torpe!

Her titi claims...

Su titi afirma que...

She's too LOUD!

¡Es muy RUIDOSA!

Even Mami sometimes says...

Incluso Mami a veces dice que....

She's too messy!

¡Es muy desordenada!

But Abuela says...

Pero Abuela dice...

Ya, she just has
TOO much **wepa**!

¡Ya, es que tiene
demasiada **wepa**!

Wepa is the song everyone loves at the barbeque; it's the magic that makes your spirit shine and your hips shake.

Wepa es la canción que todo el mundo adora en la parrillada; es la magia que hace que tu espíritu brille y tus caderas tiemblen.

But **wepa** can also be a vase slipping through your fingers, a broken mess, forgiveable mistakes.

Pero **wepa** también puede ser un vaso que se escapa de las manos, un jarrón roto o errores perdonables.

I'm sorry!

¡Perdón!

Mia loves her **wepa**.
Even if she's the only one who does.

Mia ama su **wepa**. Aunque sea la única que lo hace.

Having too much **wepa** means Mia needs somewhere for it to go. Mami tries to help by taking her to ballet class.

Tener demasiada **wepa** significa que Mia necesita un lugar donde ir. Mami intenta ayudarla llevándola a clases de ballet.

Mia tries s t r e t c h i n g her **wepa** out, but her stretches turns into f l i p s.

Mia intenta e s t i r a r su **wepa**, pero sus estiramientos se convierten en v o l t e r e t a s.

She attempts to plié
it out, but her pliés
become splits.

Intenta hacer un plié,
pero sus pliés se
convierten en splits.

No matter how hard she tries she can't seem to get her **wepa** under control.

Por mucho que lo intente, parece que no puede controlar su **wepa**.

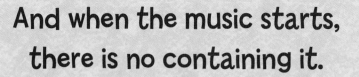

And when the music starts,
there is no containing it.

Y cuando empieza la música,
no hay quien la contenga.

Mia begins to wonder if having too much **wepa** isn't such a good thing...

Mia empieza a preguntarse si tener
tanta **wepa** no es algo tan bueno...

...until she hears a curious, familiar sound.

...hasta que escucha un sonido curioso y familiar.

Mia can't believe her eyes.
It is an entire class full of **wepa!**

Mia no puede creer lo que ven sus ojos.
¡Es una clase entera llena de **wepa**!

Mia spins with her **wepa**.
She shimmies her **wepa**.
She shakes out her **wepa**.

Mia gira con su **wepa**.
Contonea su **wepa**.
Agita su **wepa**.

No one tells her to slow down
or that she is too much.

Nadie le dice que se calme
o que es demasiada.

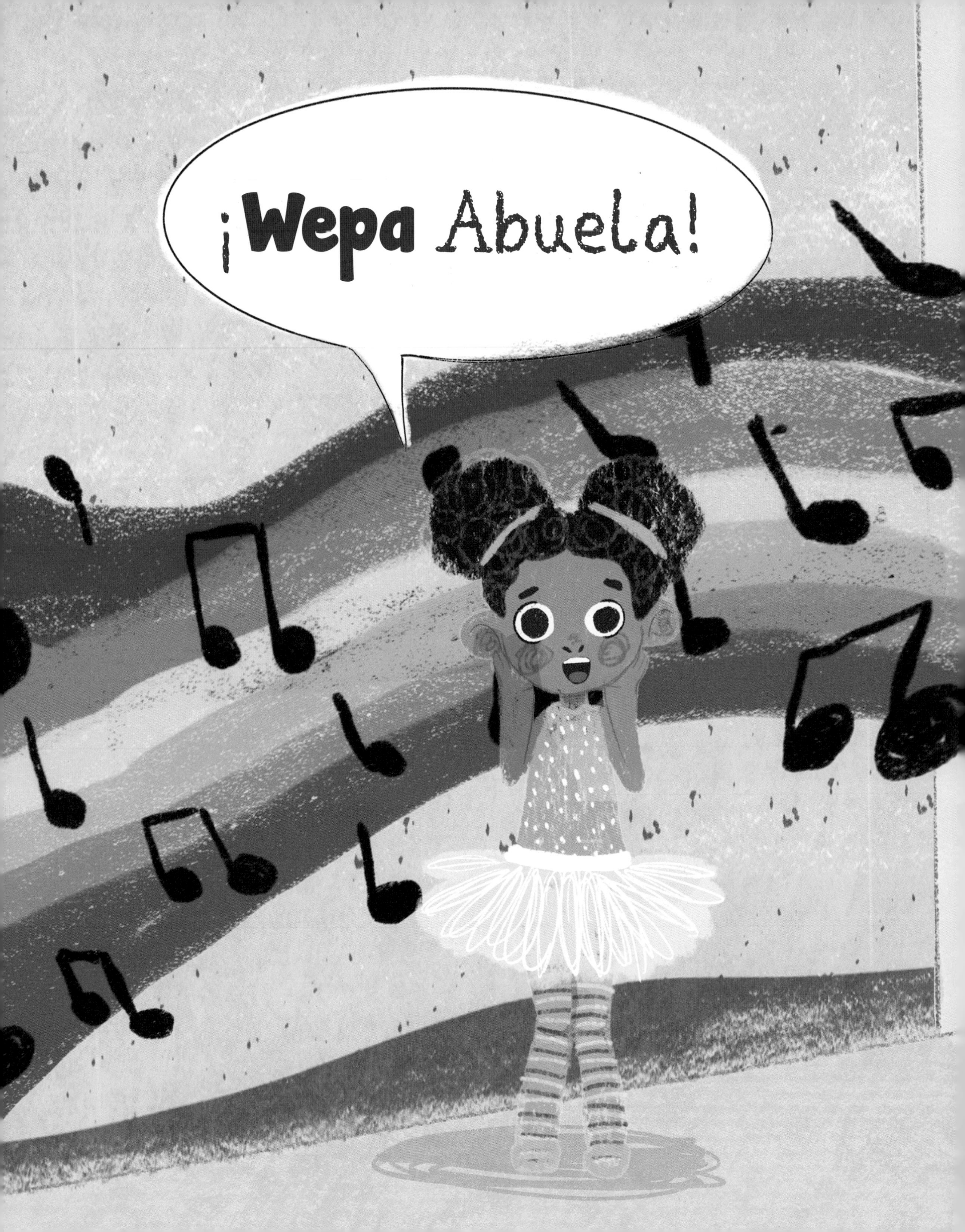
¡Wepa Abuela!

Mia has found the perfect place for her **wepa** to go.

Mia ha encontrado el lugar perfecto para dejar brillar su **wepa**.

Wepa was written to celebrate the triumphs and struggles of my family. Both my children, my husband, and I have ADHD, and as you can imagine, this creates a lot of **wepa** in our home.

We're fortunate to be in a positive place that serves our children well, but understand not everyone is there yet.

Wepa is a reminder that not all children can function in a world so rigidly structured, and they shouldn't be punished for it.

Wepa is also a gentle reminder to dismantle "chancla culture" and all that entails. We can be better. We can learn better. We can build the world to make space for **ALL** children.

*ADHD stands for attention-deficit hyperactivity disorder. It is a medical condition. A person with ADHD has differences in brain development and activity that affect attention, the ability to sit still, and self-control.